English Practice Year 6

Question Book

Giles Clare

Name _____

Schofield&Sims

Introduction

The **Schofield & Sims English Practice Year 6 Question Book** uses step-by-step practice to develop children's understanding of key English concepts. It covers every Year 6 objective in the 2014 National Curriculum programme of study.

The structure

This book is split into units, which are based on the key areas of the English curriculum for Year 6. These are:

- Grammar
- Punctuation
- Spelling
- Vocabulary
- Reading comprehension.

Each double-page spread follows a consistent 'Practise', 'Extend' and 'Apply' sequence designed to deepen and reinforce learning. Each objective also includes a 'Remember' box that reminds children of the key information needed to help answer the questions.

There are three reading comprehension units in this book. Each reading comprehension unit is linked by an overarching theme and includes a fiction, non-fiction and poetry text. Each text is accompanied by a set of comprehension questions, which practise reading skills such as inference, retrieval, summarising, prediction and analysis of word choice. The final reading comprehension unit challenges the children further by introducing the skill of comparison between two different types of text – a fiction text and a poem.

Additionally, a 'Writing skills' section allows children to apply the skills they have developed throughout the book in an extended writing task. The writing task is inspired by the themes covered in the reading comprehension texts and gives opportunities for children to showcase their creative writing.

At the back of the book, there is a 'Final practice' section. Here, mixed questions are used to check children's understanding of the knowledge and skills acquired throughout the book and identify any areas that need to be revisited.

A mastery approach

The **Primary Practice English** series follows a knowledge-based mastery approach. The books have a focus on learning with purpose to improve children's ability across all areas of English and to link learning in grammar, punctuation, spelling, vocabulary, reading and writing. There is frequent, varied practice and application of concepts to improve children's confidence when using their skills. A strong emphasis is given to vocabulary enrichment, reading for pleasure and reading stamina.

Assessment and checking progress

A 'Final practice' section is provided at the end of this book to check progress against the Year 6 English objectives. Children are given a target time of 45 minutes to complete this section, which is marked out of 30. Once complete, it enables them to assess their new knowledge and skills independently and to see the areas where they might need more practice.

Online answers

Answers for every question in this book are available to download from the **Schofield & Sims** website. The answers are accompanied by detailed explanations where helpful. There is also a progress chart, allowing children to track their learning as they complete each set of questions, and an editable certificate.

Contents

Active and passive sentences

 Practise

(1) Tick to show whether each sentence is active or passive.

Sentence	Active	Passive
a. The old oak tree fell over during last night's storm.		
b. An award for bravery was presented to Ben's dog, Sandy.		
c. The world record is broken by the up-and-coming athlete.		

(2) Underline the active or passive verb form in each sentence. It may be more than one word.

a. Our garden has been covered in snow this morning.

b. Jane Austen wrote many famous novels, including *Pride and Prejudice*.

c. Thanks to a news broadcast, Simone had heard about the closed bridge.

 Extend

(3) Rewrite these sentences in the active voice.

a. The juicy bone was gnawed by the large dog.

_____

b. Our house will be painted by the decorators tomorrow.

_____

c. The last of the iced buns has been eaten by Lottie's friend.

_____

4 Rewrite these sentences in the passive voice.

a. The rangers protect elephants and rhinos from poachers.

_____

b. That crafty fox has stolen one of my chickens.

_____

c. Something is trampling on my flowerbeds during the night.

_____

d. Megan has found Cathy's lost necklace.

_____

e. A gang of hungry raiders attacked the desert fort.

_____

Apply

5 Write **two** active sentences of your own using a subject, verb and object.

a. _____

_____

b. _____

_____

6 Rewrite your active sentences in the passive voice.

a. _____

_____

b. _____

_____

Tip Think about which part of your sentence will have the action 'done' to it.

The subjunctive form

 Practise

1 Circle the subjunctive verb in each sentence.

a. If it were my decision, we would delay our meeting.

b. She wished that the rain be over in time for the fair.

c. They ask that she provide an answer at her earliest convenience.

d. We request that he sign the letter after reading its contents.

e. He was behaving as if he were delighted about it.

f. The doctor suggested I take some medicine for my sore throat.

g. Were I able to time-travel, I would visit ancient Rome.

2 Underline the clauses that contain subjunctive verbs in this passage.

> My family and I are all hoping to escape to the seaside next week. If I were in charge of the weather, it would be sunny all week as I hope to spend most of my time surfing. My father suggested that we be on the road early on Friday morning, but my little brother is busy. According to my mother, it is essential he go to his violin lesson! I proposed that he give it up, but my mother said I was being impatient. If it weren't for him, we would get to the beach sooner.

Tip Identify the verbs in the passage and decide whether they are different to how they usually appear in the present tense.

3 Write the correct subjunctive verb to complete each sentence. Use each word once.

pay	have	were	set	be

a. I suggest she _____ off now to catch the train.

b. He looked as if he _____ about to fall over.

c. We ask that you _____ on time for the meeting.

d. He proposed that he _____ another week to do his homework.

e. They demanded she _____ for the damage.

4 Write the underlined verbs in the subjunctive form.

a. If he <u>was</u> thinking clearly, he would agree with you.   _____

b. He suggested she <u>takes</u> a jumper with her for later.   _____

c. It is vital that he <u>comes</u> to the house immediately.   _____

d. We demand that the parcel <u>is</u> delivered on time today.   _____

e. She cried in alarm as though she <u>was</u> facing a poisonous spider.   _____

Apply

5 Use your own ideas to complete these sentences. Use the subjunctive form in your answer.

a. If _____, I would have two birthdays a year!

b. I have proposed that he _____.

c. It is essential that she _____.

d. The owner demanded that the _____.

e. They suggested that she _____.

Multipart sentences

Long sentences may contain multiple main and subordinate clauses, phrases and adverbials. It is important to identify the main clause or clauses to gain a basic idea of the meaning of the sentence. For example: 'Under cover of darkness, **the spy**, who was exhausted, **entered the base**'. The main clause is in **bold**.

 Practise

(1) Cross out everything in these sentences that is not part of the main clause.

   a. From tomorrow, I will go jogging every day, whatever the weather.

   b. The bus, which was packed with excited holidaymakers, came to a sudden stop in the middle of nowhere.

   c. What made things worse was that she had missed breakfast because she had woken up extremely late.

   d. With a single flip of the coin, his life, which was normally so boring, changed forever.

 Extend

(2) Underline the main clauses and circle the subordinate clauses in these sentences.

   a. The old man, who walked with the help of a cane, crossed the sunny park and fed the pigeons.

   b. We left after lunch, which was later than we had planned, and drove to our next hotel, where we were greeted by a grumpy gardener.

   c. As dusk settled over the hills, Thomas set off on his adventure, which he had been looking forward to for so long.

   d. Although Amy hadn't realised it yet, her actions would have consequences that would come back to haunt her and she would be filled with regret.

3 Underline all the adverbials in each sentence, then circle the types of adverbials used.

   a. Before long, Callum was reading a new book every few days on his bed.

     adverbial(s) of time   adverbial(s) of place   adverbial(s) of manner

   b. Obviously angry, my brother threw his controller on the sofa and disappeared upstairs.

     adverbial(s) of time   adverbial(s) of place   adverbial(s) of manner

> **Tip** An adverbial of time describes when something happens. An adverbial of place describes where it happens. An adverbial of manner describes how it happens.

Apply

4 Use your own ideas to complete these sentences.

   a. Last week, _____ , Mika collected some berries,

     which _____ .

   b. _____ , although Layla was exhausted,

     _____ and

     _____ slowly.

   c. Whenever _____ ,

     _____ .

5 Write **three** multipart sentences of your own using main and subordinate clauses as well as a range of adverbials.

   a. _____

     _____

   b. _____

     _____

   c. _____

     _____

Layout devices

 Practise

(1) Label the layout devices in this text. Use the labels in the box.

table   subheading   heading   bullet point list   column headings

1960s Youth Fashion •—— a. _____

In the 1960s, lots of young people dressed in one of two different styles.

Mods •— b. _____

Mods rode scooters and cut their hair in a 'bowl cut'. They wore:

- slim, smart suits
- formal shoes   c. _____
- khaki-green parka coats.

Rockers

Rocker fashion was centred around their love of motorcycles. They wore their hair with a quiff at the front. Rockers wore:

- straight-legged jeans
- black leather jackets
- motorcycle boots.   d. _____

Mod music	Rocker music
The Who, The Yardbirds, Small Faces	Eddie Cochran, Bo Diddley, Gene Vincent

e. _____

Extend

2 Tick to show the most suitable subheading for this paragraph. Tick **one**.

> By 2005, many mobile phones had built-in digital cameras. Sales of camera phones overtook sales of film or digital cameras. Touchscreen phones also became much more popular than phones with keypads when Apple launched its first iPhone® in 2007.

Smartphone touchscreens ☐

The end of cameras ☐

The development of mobile phones ☐

Apply

3 Here is a passage of jumbled-up information about a famous mountain. Rewrite these sentences using layout devices to organise them and make their meaning clearer.

> The Matterhorn is in Switzerland. Many early attempts to climb it failed. Matterhorn means 'meadow peak' in Swiss-German. In 1865, a British climber led a party of seven climbers to the summit via the north face. Tragically, four of them fell and died on the way back down. It is easier to reach the summit today. Climbers use a cable car and then ropes and ladders to get to the peak. The Matterhorn is 4478 metres tall. About 3000 people climb the mountain every year, but it is still dangerous.

_____

_____

_____

_____

_____

_____

Adverbials for cohesion

Remember

'Cohesion' means how well a text links together. Adverbials can be used to link points within paragraphs, or to link different paragraphs in the same text. Different types of adverbials are used for different purposes, such as sequencing time, comparing and contrasting, or emphasising or summarising a point.

 ## Practise

(1) Sort these adverbials into the table according to their purpose.

| equally | as a result | therefore | lastly | although | firstly |

Time or sequencing	Comparing or contrasting	Emphasising or summarising

 ## Extend

(2) Underline the adverbials that help build cohesion in this text.

Plastic is made from petrochemicals, which are not renewable. Some plastics can be recycled, although it is estimated that only one-fifth of all plastics in the world are recycled. As a consequence, millions of plastic products pollute the environment.

On the other hand, plastics can be very useful. Firstly, they are easy to mould, so they can be used for many purposes. Secondly, cars have more plastic parts now, making them lighter and, as a result, more fuel-efficient. In addition, manufacturers say that making plastics only consumes 4% of the world's oil production.

Despite this, it is vital that we produce less plastic and recycle more.

 **Apply**

(3) Complete this story using the adverbials in the box. Use each word or phrase once.

just then	in the distance	slowly	now or never	just like normal
the next day	whenever	in exasperation	to my surprise
impatiently	into the lounge	usually

That first morning, everything seemed fine. _____,

I picked up the lead and called Scruff for his walk.

_____, our old dog jumps up from his basket straight

away, wagging his tail, _____ it's time for 'walkies'.

"Come on, Scruff," I said _____. "It's walkies

_____. I've got school soon."

This time, as I stood in the hall waiting, he didn't appear. Then, just as I was about to call

him again, I noticed him peering around the door.

_____, he emerged, his eyes fixed on the front door.

_____, he was shaking and his ears were flat on his

head. I reached out to attach the lead to his collar, but he turned tail and scampered away

_____.

_____, I tried again. However, it was the same story.

Scruff stuck his nose into the hall, whimpered and disappeared.

"Not again! What's the problem?" I said _____.

_____, I had a weird sensation. The hairs on the

back of my neck stood up. Then, _____, I heard a

high-pitched shriek.

Audience and purpose

The audience is the type of person a piece of writing is aimed at. The purpose is the reason that an author is writing. For example, an author can write to inform, to persuade or to entertain.

A text can be written in different styles depending on the words used. Some writing is formal and other writing is informal. Writing can also make the reader feel different things depending on the effect that the writer wishes to create.

Always think about the audience and purpose of a text to help with choosing the correct style and structure when writing.

 Practise

(1) Tick to show the most likely audience and purpose for each text. Tick **one** in each column.

a. The Galapagos Islands, which are located in the Pacific Ocean, were formed by volcanoes. Some of the volcanoes are still active. Habitats on the islands range from rocky cliffs to deserts to sandy beaches. Animals have adapted to the different island habitats over the centuries.

Audience:

a four year old ☐

an 11 year old ☐

Purpose:

to inform ☐

to persuade ☐

b. Giant Tortoise said, "It's too hot today!"

His friend, Green Iguana, said, "Oh dear! I like swimming when it's hot. Come for a swim with me."

Giant Tortoise looked sad. He didn't want to go for a swim.

Audience:

a student studying history ☐

a child reading a picture book ☐

Purpose:

to instruct ☐

to entertain ☐

▶ Extend

2 Write the likely audience and purpose for each text, then circle the style and effect created.

a. The delayed delivery is totally unacceptable, and your company is entirely at fault. Please deliver the goods immediately or refund the amount in full.

Audience: _____ **Purpose:** _____

Style: formal   informal   **Effect:**   friendly   serious

b. Explain your choices for audience and style in **Question 2a**.

_____

_____

c. Who's hungry? Try our new app for free local deliveries. No fuss, just food!

Audience: _____ **Purpose:** _____

Style: formal   informal   **Effect:**   friendly   serious

d. Explain your choices for purpose and effect in **Question 2c**.

_____

_____

☁ Apply

3 Create a short piece of writing of your own. Choose and circle an audience, purpose, style and effect from below to focus your writing.

Audience: a 10 year old   an adult   **Purpose:**   to persuade   to instruct

Style: formal   informal   **Effect:**   friendly   serious

_____

_____

_____

Colons

 Practise

1 Circle the colon that is in the correct place in each sentence.

   a. Mackenzie's dad : was excited : Mackenzie was performing : on stage : for the first time.

   b. It was still dark : when they arrived : Martha had insisted : on leaving : at 3 o'clock.

   c. The football match : was abandoned : during a sudden storm, : lightning struck : the floodlights.

   d. I would like : these presents : for my birthday : a new bike, a pair of jeans and : some slippers.

2 Circle the colon that is in the correct place in each sentence, then write what each colon is introducing.

   a. I have several : favourite meals : fish and chips, : katsu chicken curry : and roast lamb.

     This colon is introducing _____.

   b. Third : Little Pig : Unlike you, : I shall make : my house of brick!

     This colon is introducing _____.

   c. For example: 'simple' : is an : antonym of : 'difficult'.

     This colon is introducing _____.

   d. Anne Frank : wrote : "Whoever is happy : will make : others happy too."

     This colon is introducing _____.

▶ Extend

3 Insert a colon in the correct place in each sentence.

a. Take a look at this example 48 ÷ 2 = 24, so 48 ÷ 20 = 2.4.

b. As Thomas Edison famously said "I failed my way to success."

c. King Richard III A horse, a horse, my kingdom for a horse!

4 Insert a colon in the correct place in each sentence.

a. Tonight was a waste of time nobody showed up and the meeting had to be postponed.

b. Ollie was really cross for good reason Ruby, his sister, had broken his brand new games console.

c. Adanna missed her bus this morning for some reason, her alarm clock didn't go off.

Apply

5 Write **one** sentence of your own that uses a colon to introduce a list about hobbies.

_____

_____

6 Use your own ideas to complete these sentences by writing a first or second clause.

a. My mum was delighted: _____.

b. At a glance, they looked like twins: _____.

c. _____: Stanley had flooded the bathroom.

d. _____: Tilly was late for rehearsal again.

Semicolons

 Practise

1. Circle the semicolon that is in the correct place in each sentence.

   a. Harriet was tall ; for her age ; Eve was shorter ; than average.

   b. The roads are really icy ; this morning ; you should delay ; your journey ; if possible.

   c. The damage ; had been done ; nothing was going ; to improve ; the situation.

2. Complete these lists by writing a colon or semicolon in the correct places.

   a. I really love watching these types of films __ superhero films with lots of

   action __ crime thrillers full of suspense __ and silly comedy films, in which the

   animals talk and behave badly.

   b. You will need the following ingredients __ two fillets of salmon, which should be

   as fresh as possible __ 100g of egg noodles per person __ three-quarters of a litre

   of vegetable stock __ a bunch of spring onions __ and half a bottle of teriyaki sauce.

» Extend

3. Insert a semicolon in the correct place in each sentence.

   a. Overnight, there will be a powerful storm tomorrow, the rain will ease.

   b. Amina practises piano every day her brother, Ade, never picks up his trumpet.

   c. In Devon, it's cream then jam on scones in Cornwall, it's jam then cream.

4 Insert colons and semicolons in the correct places in these sentences.

a. Here is today's itinerary breakfast in the canteen abseiling at the climbing tower for two hours lunch around the campfire rock pooling, fossil hunting and sandcastle building on the beach and finally, the evening talent show.

b. There are many options to choose from an extra comfy seat, which comes with a pillow free snacks in the lounge a pair of noise-cancelling headphones or more storage room for your bags.

Apply

5 Use your own ideas to complete these sentences by writing a second clause after the semicolon.

a. Suzie adores horses and ponies; _____

_____.

b. Today, it has been grey outside; _____

_____.

c. My favourite sport is rounders; _____

_____.

d. Oscar had made up his mind; _____

_____.

6 Use your own ideas to complete these lists. Use semicolons to separate the items.

a. I did several things during half-term: _____

_____

_____

b. I have lots of plans for the future: _____

_____

_____

Hyphens and dashes

Hyphens join words together to make compound nouns, adjectives and verbs. They make the meaning clear. For example: '**merry-go-round**'.

A dash separates two independent clauses, often in more informal writing. For example: 'The alarm didn't go off – he'd be late!' A dash is longer than a hyphen.

 Practise

(1) Tick to show the correct position of the dash in each of these sentences.

a. The ground trembled – beneath their feet – it was another – aftershock.

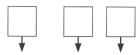

b. We have the most exciting news – to tell – you – it will have to wait though!

c. Jackson was cold and fed up – his bike tyre – had punctured – on the way home.

(2) Insert hyphens to make **one** compound word in each of these sentences, then circle the type of compound word they make.

a. The villagers were worried about the man eating tiger near the farm.

This is a compound **noun / adjective / verb**.

b. Joe and Tom ice skated for an hour without falling over.

This is a compound **noun / adjective / verb**.

c. The police took a statement from my sister in law to discover what had happened.

This is a compound **noun / adjective / verb**.

Tip Read the sentences aloud to identify where words may naturally want to join together. Hyphens might be missing from these places.

3 Underline the last word of the first clause and the first word of the second clause in each of these sentences. Insert a dash in the correct place between the two clauses. One has been done for you.

    a. My cat begs for more after her <u>breakfast</u> — <u>she</u> must love her new cat food.

    b. Alyssa suddenly sneezed loudly it was hay fever time of year again!

    c. The water looked clear and inviting Isaac couldn't wait to get in.

4 Insert hyphens in the correct places in these sentences.

    a. My mother in law is a spy with a cupboard full of high tech gadgets.

    b. Ben's five year old sister is left handed.

    c. This time saving machine will help you produce tasty, deep fried treats!

 Apply

5 Rewrite this passage using hyphens in the correct places.

> This is Channel Ninety Nine News, the home of the most up to date, fastest moving stories of the day. First, news of a break in at a free range chicken farm last night. A blonde haired, middle aged man was spotted outside the gates by a passer by. Two hours later, during a spot check, guards discovered a smashed third floor window. They then realised that two hundred and thirty five chickens were missing.

_____

_____

_____

_____

_____

Ellipses and dashes

Remember

An ellipsis (**...**) can represent either words that have been missed out or a pause for effect. The pause might create tension or indicate an unfinished thought. A dash (**–**) can also be used for effect. It can show an interruption or a change of thought or speech.

 Practise

1 Draw lines to match the example with the correct definition.

"You took my ball and –" "That's not true!"	ellipsis to show an unfinished thought
The front door to the creepy house creaked open slowly ...	dash to show a change in the direction of speech or thought
The girl ... finally arrived home.	dash to show interruption
No-one had lived at the farm for years – or so he thought.	ellipsis to show omitted words
"I can't believe that you ..."	ellipsis to show tension

 Extend

2 Rewrite this sentence using an ellipsis to replace the underlined words.

The children <u>who had been picked to perform</u> put on an amazing show.

_____

3 Rewrite this sentence using an ellipsis to create tension.

The explorer pulled back the curtain of vines and peered inside.

_____

4 Rewrite this sentence using a dash to show a change in direction of speech or thought.

That strange noise outside is just an animal or is it?

_____

5 Rewrite these sentences using an ellipsis to show an unfinished thought.

"What did you see?" asked Zac.

"I really don't," replied Molly, her eyes wide with shock.

_____

_____

6 Rewrite these sentences using a dash to show an interruption.

Zac asked, "What did you see?"

"I really don't want to talk about it!" snapped Molly.

_____

_____

Apply

7 Write **four** sentences of your own using an ellipsis or a dash in the different ways described in the **Practise** section. You could use direct speech.

a. _____

_____

b. _____

_____

c. _____

_____

d. _____

_____

Bullet points

 Practise

1 **a.** Here are two similar bullet point lists. Circle all the punctuation and capital letters in both lists.

i. My favourite types of video game are:

- multiplayer building games
- casual puzzlers
- cartoon platformers
- fantasy adventures.

ii. My favourite types of video game are:

- Multiplayer building games;
- casual puzzlers.
- Cartoon platformers;
- fantasy adventures

b. Which of the lists (**i** or **ii**) uses punctuation most consistently? _____

2 **a.** Here are two similar bullet point lists. Circle all the punctuation and capital letters in both lists.

i. here are some facts about Russia

- it is the largest country in the world
- It has around 100 000 rivers;
- three out of four Russians live in cities;
- Children go to school from age six.

ii. Here are some facts about Russia.

- It is the largest country in the world.
- It has around 100 000 rivers.
- Three out of four Russians live in cities.
- Children go to school from age six.

b. Which of the lists (**i** or **ii**) uses punctuation most consistently? _____

c. Why do the bullet points end with full stops in list **ii**?

_____

_____

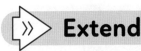 **Extend**

3 Rewrite this bullet point list using the correct punctuation.

here is some advice for driving in snowy conditions

- decide whether your journey is necessary

  fit your car with winter tyres;

- take a blanket and mobile-phone charger in case you get stuck

  let someone know when you are expecting to arrive.

_____

_____

_____

_____

_____

_____

Apply

4 Rewrite this text to turn it into a bullet point list.

Hiking trip equipment a pair of sturdy boots a warm top a waterproof jacket a compass a whistle for emergencies

_____

_____

_____

_____

_____

_____

Tip If there is a full sentence on every bullet point, each sentence needs a full stop. Single nouns or noun phrases should only have a full stop after the last item in the list.

Prefixes

Remember

A prefix is usually added directly to the beginning of a root word or base word to change its meaning. For example: '**dis**appear' has the opposite meaning to 'appear'. In some cases, a hyphen is needed when adding a prefix. For example, '**re**-examine' not '**re**examine'.

Practise

(1) Tick to show where the hyphen is used to join the prefix correctly.

co-exist ☐   im-mortal ☐   semi-detached ☐

sub-marine ☐   ir-regular ☐   re-enact ☐

(2) Draw lines to match each prefix in the outer cloud to the correct base words in the inner cloud. One has been done for you.

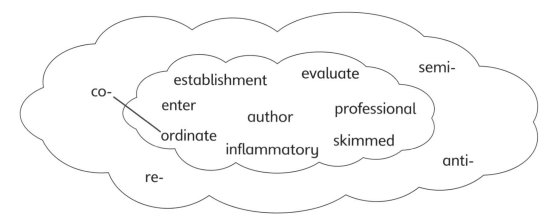

Extend

(3) Underline the words that need hyphens in these sentences, then write the word with the correct spelling.

a. My mum and my aunt coown a cosmetics business.   _____

b. He remained friends with his exwife.   _____

c. In selfdefence classes, you learn to keep yourself safe.   _____

d. The archaeologists discovered a preViking burial mound.   _____

(4) Rewrite these sentences using hyphens in the correct places.

a. A tourist has dis-appeared in subSaharan Africa.

_____

b. Mandeep is my coworker at the super-market.

_____

c. Anna mis-judged the penalty in the semifinal.

_____

d. The in-active satellite reentered the atmosphere.

_____

Tip Identify the prefixes in the words and decide whether they need a hyphen.

Apply

(5) Write **four** sentences of your own using each of the hyphenated words from the box.

| re-examine | ultra-ambitious | co-operate | pre-existing |

a. _____

_____

b. _____

_____

c. _____

_____

d. _____

_____

Suffixes

Remember

A suffix is a letter or letter string 'fixed' on to the end of a word to make a new one. The suffixes –ible and –able make adjectives, and the suffixes –ibly and –ably make adverbs. For example: 'bend**able**' and 'sens**ibly**'.

When a suffix is added to words ending in 'fer', double the 'r' when the 'fer' syllable is stressed. For example: 'refer' becomes 'refer**ring**', or 'refer**ence**' depending on which syllable is stressed.

 ## Practise

1 Circle the adjectives that have the suffix –able or –ible.

comfortable   bible   responsible   sensible   cable   edible

invisible   disable   audible   fable   syllable   respectable

2 Change each of these –able and –ible adjectives into adverbs using the suffix –ly.

a. understandable   _____

b. visible   _____

c. terrible   _____

d. notable   _____

3 Circle the correct spellings in these sentences.

a. The football player asked to be **transferred / transfered** to a different club.

b. I like coffee but my **preferrence / preference** is always a nice cup of tea!

c. The villagers made an **offerring / offering** to their ancient gods.

d. What is the **difference / differrence** between twenty-six and forty-two?

e. The thief **pilferred / pilfered** some coins from my pocket.

Extend

4 Change these root words into adjectives by adding –ible or –able, or adverbs by adding –ibly or –ably. Sometimes the spelling of the root word changes when you add a suffix.

Root word	Add –ible or –able		Root word	Add –ibly or –ably
a. convert			**d.** horror	
b. adore			**e.** memory	
c. rely			**f.** suit	

5 Complete each word by adding an appropriate suffix so that the sentence makes sense.

a. The athlete was suffer_____ from an injury and missed the race.

b. In comprehension, 'reading between the lines' is known as making infer_____.

c. The team confer_____ about who should be chosen as the new captain.

d. Colette refer_____ to the dictionary to check the correct spelling of the word.

Apply

6 Complete this text by adding suffixes to the words in the box. Use each word once.

> sense   reason   terror   rely   accept
> irritate   consider   understand   notice   comfort

My mum thinks it is r_____ to only give me 20p more pocket money

each week when I help with the housework. That's not a n_____

increase! It's t_____ and not a _____. It would be

u_____ if I were not r_____, but I put

c_____ effort into my chores! All I want is a pair of stylish,

c_____ trainers instead of my s_____ shoes.

The whole thing makes me really i_____!

Base words and root words

Remember

A base word has a meaning on its own. Its meaning changes when a prefix, a suffix or both is added. For example: '**act**' and 're**act**'. A root word does not mean anything in English on its own: a prefix or suffix is added to give it meaning. For example: '**therm**' and '**therm**ometer'. A word formed from a root word is called a derivative.

Practise

(1) Underline the base word in each of the words in the cloud. Circle any prefixes and put a box around any suffixes. One has been done for you.

Ⓥepayable   misheard   treatment   unhelpful

sailor   deformity   useless   depart

disagreeable   accessible   fastest   multiplayer

(2) Add a prefix, a suffix or both to each of these root words to make a new word. Use each root word once.

dia   aero   chron   bene   hypo   spect

_____   _____   _____

_____   _____   _____

Extend

(3) Add a prefix, a suffix or both to each of these base words to make a new word. Do not use suffixes that alter the spelling of the base word. Use each base word once.

happy   care   view   civil   sense   cycle   norm   break   point

_____   _____   _____

_____   _____   _____

_____   _____   _____

4 Write as many derivatives as you can for each of these root words, using the words in brackets as a clue.

a. hydr (water) _____

b. naut (ship) _____

c. lev (lift) _____

d. dyna (power) _____

Apply

5 Complete this crossword using the clues and the base or root words shown.

Across
2. to deal with something badly (verb)
3. to get out (verb)
5. farming (noun)
7. to send a signal (verb)

Down
1. someone who investigates something (noun)
4. a device for making your voice louder (noun)
5. next to each other (adjective)
6. an old machine for writing letters (noun)

Homophones

Remember

Homophones are words that sound the same but have different spellings and meanings. For example: 'cereal' and 'serial'. Some homophones sound the same and have similar meanings but have slightly different endings. Homophones ending in 'ce' are nouns; those ending in 'se' are verbs. For example: 'practi**ce**' (noun) and 'practi**se**' (verb).

Practise

(1) Circle the correct homophones so that these sentences make sense.

a. After the long **ascent / assent**, the climber was **wary / weary**.

b. One **principal / principle** of business is to make a **prophet / profit**.

c. The following **mourning / morning**, the train was still **stationary / stationery**.

d. The adventurer sensed danger and did not want to **proceed / precede** any **farther / father**.

(2) Sort these homophones into the correct boxes.

devise	licence	advise	license	practice	advice	device	practise

Nouns	**Verbs**

Tip Think about the ending of each word to decide whether it is a noun or verb. Are there any patterns that you recognise?

Extend

3 Write the correct meaning of each of these homophones. The word class is given in brackets.

a. affect   (verb)   _____

b. effect   (noun)   _____

c. compliment   (noun)   _____

d. complement   (verb)   _____

e. descent   (noun)   _____

f. dissent   (verb)   _____

4 Circle the correct spellings in each sentence.

a. She **advised** / **adviced** him on how to make the most of his new **devise** / **device**.

b. He **deviced** / **devised** a clever plan to **licence** / **license** his invention for sale.

c. Please take my **advice** / **advise** and go to the doctor's **practise** / **practice** as soon as possible.

d. I need to **practise** / **practice** a lot more before I do the test to get my driver's **licence** / **license**.

 Apply

5 Use your own ideas to complete these sentences. Use **one** of the homophones from the **Practise** section in each sentence.

a. The old man _____.

b. Give me _____.

c. Jamila _____.

d. We must _____.

Synonyms and antonyms

 ## Practise

1 Draw lines to match the words to their synonyms and antonyms. One has been done for you.

Synonym	Word	Antonym
condemn	difficult	deceitful
honest	criticise	professional
challenging	amateur	compliment
hindrance	sincere	pleasure
beginner	nuisance	straightforward

Tip You could check the meaning of the words in a dictionary before matching them to their synonym and antonym.

 ## Extend

2 Complete each sentence using the synonym of the underlined word from the box. Use each word once.

> occasionally   perfect   explanation   accomplished

a. The runner <u>finished</u> the marathon and _____ her dream.

b. We <u>sometimes</u> go to Cornwall and _____ eat fish and chips by the sea.

c. Toby spoke _____ Japanese and his writing was <u>flawless</u>.

d. The first boy gave his <u>account</u> and then the other boy offered his _____.

3 Write the antonyms for these words using the prefixes in the box.

> un   dis   im   in   il   ir

a. convenience _____

b. available _____

c. responsible _____

d. practical _____

e. advantage _____

f. logical _____

Apply

4 Rewrite this paragraph, using synonyms to replace the underlined words. Try to make it sound more interesting.

> The spy waited in the <u>hot</u>, <u>dark</u> room. Sweat <u>ran</u> down his back. He had been <u>hiding</u> for hours, and was <u>tired</u> and <u>hungry</u>. He would have to <u>take</u> the first <u>chance</u> to escape. <u>Suddenly</u>, he <u>noticed</u> footsteps. Someone was <u>walking</u> towards the door!

_____

_____

_____

_____

5 Rewrite this paragraph, using antonyms to replace the underlined words to change the meaning and feeling of the story.

> Dr Ruin's bodyguard was <u>suspicious</u> and <u>vicious</u> by nature. He didn't know why, but everything about their meeting felt <u>wrong</u>. It was a <u>sombre</u> occasion. Dr Ruin was explaining how his plans had been <u>ruined</u> by a <u>meddling</u> spy. The bodyguard was <u>furious</u>.

_____

_____

_____

_____

Figurative language

Remember

Figurative language, including metaphors, similes and idioms, is language that does not have its normal, literal meaning. It can enhance or emphasise meaning. Metaphors describe something as something else. For example: 'The sun **is** a golden ball'.
Similes describe something as being 'like' something else. For example: 'Kim was **as** strong **as** an ox'. Idioms are phrases that have well-known, non-literal meanings. For example: 'Ben felt **under the weather**' meaning 'Ben felt **ill**'.

Practise

1. Tick to show whether these sentences are metaphors, similes or idioms. Some sentences may be more than one.

Sentence	Metaphor	Simile	Idiom
a. The moon was a silver plate in the night sky.			
b. Reading is a gateway to other worlds.			
c. Her face was as red as a beetroot.			
d. My sister has a singing voice like an angel.			
e. He was putty in her hands.			

Extend

2. Complete these similes and metaphors using the words in the box.

> bears   chasm   coin   lambs

a. The fluffy clouds were like excited _____ racing across the sky.

b. Their disagreement was a deep _____ between them.

c. My twin brothers are as bad-tempered as _____ when they are hungry.

d. The sun was a copper _____ resting on the horizon.

3 Complete these idioms using the words in the box, then match them to their meanings. Use each word once. One has been done for you.

> gauntlet ~~dogs~~ square spill

a. Let sleeping ___dogs___ lie. Set a challenge.

b. Go back to _____ one. Avoid restarting an argument.

c. _____ the beans. Start at the beginning.

d. Throw down the _____. Give away a secret.

Apply

4 Write the meaning of these idioms.

a. I've got a bone to pick with you.

_____

b. She is always blowing her own trumpet.

_____

c. You are making a mountain out of a molehill.

_____

d. That was a piece of cake!

_____

5 Use your own ideas to write metaphors for these things.

a. the sea

_____

b. a mountain

_____

Formal and informal language

 Practise

1 Draw lines to match these formal words to the informal words that have the same meaning.

obtain	say sorry
correct	enough
apologise	right
sufficient	get

2 Circle the formal word that means the same as the informal word in bold.

a. ask for	request	require	refuse
b. friend	antagonist	advocate	acquaintance
c. find out	determine	discover	devise
d. view	proportion	perspective	proposal

 Extend

3 This is part of an email to a friend. Circle the more informal word in each pair.

Something **comical / funny** happened on holiday. The waiter **chucked / poured** ice down the back of my **dad's / father's** neck. He **jumped up / leapt to his feet** and knocked over our whole table, **precisely / right** in the **middle / centre** of the restaurant.

④ Write the correct formal or informal word from the box to complete these sentences.

> okay   pricey   grateful   permit   expensive   acceptable   let   chuffed

a. I would be extremely _____ if you could reply to this email as soon

as is convenient.

b. Wow, that phone is a bit _____!

c. It is not _____ to forget to use capital letters for proper nouns in

your writing.

d. _____ me have a go with that, mate.

Tip Think about how formal or informal each sentence is before you choose each word.

Apply

⑤ This passage is from a letter to the local council from your class. Rewrite the passage,
replacing the underlined informal words with suitable formal ones from the box.
Use each word once.

> damage   children   hard-wearing   ensured   delighted   engaging
>
> provide   materials   consider   environment   believe   submit

We are <u>happy</u> to <u>put forward</u> our winning design for a new playground for you to

<u>think about</u>. We <u>think</u> our design will <u>make</u> a safe and <u>fun</u> space for <u>kids</u> of all ages.

We have <u>made sure</u> that all the <u>things</u> will be <u>tough</u> and will not <u>hurt</u> the <u>world</u>.

_____

_____

_____

_____

£0

Dictionary and thesaurus work

Remember

A dictionary is used to find out what words mean and to check their spelling. A thesaurus is useful for finding synonyms (for example: '**solid**' is a synonym of '**hard**'). Both are arranged with the headwords in alphabetical order. The first and last words on each page (guide words) are shown together at the top of the page.

Practise

(1) Put the following words into alphabetical order.

a. nail   myth   name   mystic   mystery   napkin

_____

b. thicken   theory   thermal   therefore   thorough   thief

_____

(2) Use a thesaurus to find **three** synonyms for each of these words. The word class is given in brackets.

a. busy (adjective)   _____   _____   _____

b. sleep (noun)   _____   _____   _____

c. cold (adjective)   _____   _____   _____

Extend

(3) The words in bold are the guide words from pages in a dictionary. Circle the words that would be found on the same page as these guide words.

a. clipper to **club**   clock   coastguard   cluck   clothing   clinic   coarse

b. luxurious to **magazine**   magnify   lunch   luxury   mackerel   lottery   magpie

c. viscount to **voice**   vivid   visible   virus   vintage   volunteer   vocalist

④ Complete the **two** missing synonyms for each of the overused adjectives in brackets.

a. He's a t_____ player with a p_____ attitude. (good)

b. Jo is always w_____ to help with a s_____ smile. (happy)

c. Alice is g_____ as she received some t_____ news. (sad)

Apply

⑤ Use a dictionary to look up these words. Write the word class or classes, then write an example sentence for each word.

a. unanimous   _____

_____

b. diligence   _____

_____

c. venture   _____

_____

d. readily   _____

_____

⑥ Rewrite this paragraph, using synonyms from a thesaurus to replace the underlined words. The passage should keep the same meaning overall.

Every day, my friendly grandpa goes for a walk in the local park. He loves sitting on the same bench, especially on a sunny morning. He reads his newspaper and feeds the noisy ducks. Once, he asked to join in a football game with some teenagers. They were surprised because he was so quick. He scored some great goals!

_____

_____

_____

_____

Year 6 word list

 Practise

1 Sort these words into the table according to their word class. Look at the suffixes to help you decide. Use a dictionary to help.

> conscience   marvellous   correspond   desperate   hindrance
> interfere   necessary   sincerely   opportunity   physical

Nouns	Adjectives	Verbs	Adverbs

Extend

2 Complete the sentences using the words in the box, then write the word class for each word. Use each word once.

> guarantee   awkward   privilege   sacrifice

a. Dad's bad joke was met by an _____ silence. _____

b. I will _____ my free time to reach my goal. _____

c. Will you _____ that you will turn up on time? _____

d. It really was a _____ to meet my sporting hero. _____

③ Write each word from the box, then draw lines to match each word to its word class and meaning. One has been done for you.

| ~~vehicle~~ | prejudice | controversy | harass | disastrous |

vehicle ———— noun   an unfair opinion

_____   verb   extremely bad or unsuccessful

_____   adjective   to annoy or upset someone

_____   noun   a major argument about something

_____   noun   a machine for transport

Apply

④ Read the words in this table. If you do not know what they mean, use a dictionary to look them up.

Nouns	Adjectives	Verbs
bruise, category, cemetery, committee, community, competition, convenience, existence, explanation, identity, neighbour, nuisance, parliament, pronunciation, restaurant, signature, variety, vegetable	aggressive, amateur, available, awkward, disastrous, familiar, foreign, individual, leisure, marvellous, necessary, physical	accompany, correspond, embarrass, guarantee, harass, interfere, interrupt, persuade, programme, queue, sacrifice

a. Write a sentence that uses **two** nouns from the table.

_____

b. Write a sentence that uses **one** noun and **one** adjective from the table.

_____

c. Write a sentence that uses **one** adjective and **two** verbs from the table.

_____

_____

Thematic language

 Practise

(1) Sort the following words into the table, then use a dictionary to check the meaning of each word.

> uncomfortable   creed   privacy   hew   discord
> compassionate   scarcely   self-evident   commotion   midst
> initial   ailment   deteriorate   artificial   disperse

Words with meanings I know	Words with meanings I can guess	Words with meanings I don't know

Tip Think about the prefixes and suffixes when you see a word you don't know. You might know the meaning of the root or base word. You might also be able to guess the word class from the suffix.

② Choose **one** word from the table with a meaning you did not know. Write a sentence using the word to show that you now understand what it means.

_____

_____

⏩ Extend

③ Write the missing letters for each word using the synonym in the brackets as a clue.

a. p __ __ digi __ __ s   (extraordinary)

b. d __ __ bel __ __ __ __   (mistrust)

c. s __ __ bol __ __ __ __   (represent)

d. __ __ fath __ __ __ __ le   (incomprehensible)

④ Write the missing letters for each word using the antonym in the brackets as a clue.

a. fl __ __ __ __ ss   (imperfect)

b. __ __ nor __ __ ce   (understanding)

c. op __ __ __ __ __ ion   (freedom)

d. __ __ t __ __ cacy   (simplicity)

💭 Apply

⑤ Complete these sentences using the words in the box. Use each word once.

resilience   refugees   perceived   equality   likeness   injustice   dappled

a. Sitting in the _____ sunlight beneath the tree, Gracie suddenly

_____ a strong _____ between the two children.

b. The _____ showed great _____ in tackling

_____ and arguing for _____.

Topic words

Remember

The vocabulary activities on these pages are linked to interesting topics across all subjects in the curriculum. Think about prefixes, suffixes and root words when working out the meanings of these words. A dictionary and thesaurus can be useful when coming across new words for the first time.

Practise

1 Sort the words into the subjects that they would most likely be used in.

| pageant | misdiagnose | millennium | territory | memorial | hemisphere |
| hamlet | buoyancy | regalia | hypochondriac | digestible | habitable |

Science	History	Geography
_____	_____	_____
_____	_____	_____
_____	_____	_____
_____	_____	_____

Extend

2 Circle the word that is closest in meaning to the word in bold.

a. **deplete**   increase   expend   expand

b. **prolonged**   extended   shortened   widened

c. **promenade**   march   sprint   stroll

d. **commemorative**   neglectful   celebratory   honourable

3 Complete these words using the clue in brackets.

a. _____ sect   (a synonym of 'cut open')

b. sabo _____   (an antonym of 'fix')

c. equil _____   (a synonym of 'balance')

d. _____ chrome   (an antonym of 'multicoloured')

Apply

4 Complete these sentences using the words in the box. Use each word once.

> independence   emergence   deferential   conceited   conference   forcible   variant

a. The scientists at the _____ discussed the _____ of a

new _____ of the virus.

b. The citizens, who were no longer willing to be _____, finally rose up

against their _____ rulers and made a _____ argument

for _____ .

Tip Revisit the **Spelling** unit in this book to review the rules and patterns for the words in these sentences.

5 Write **four** sentences of your own. Use **one** of the words from the box in each sentence.

> frieze   intractable   acrophobia   convalescence   gullible   merchandise

a. _____

b. _____

c. _____

d. _____

The Wonderful Wizard of Oz, by L. Frank Baum

The Wonderful Wizard of Oz was written by L. Frank Baum and first published in 1900. The story is about the adventures of a young girl called Dorothy in the magical land of Oz. At the start of the story, Dorothy is living with her Aunt Em and Uncle Henry on a farm in Kansas in the USA.

Suddenly Uncle Henry stood up.

"There's a cyclone coming, Em," he called to his wife. "I'll go look after the stock." Then he ran toward the sheds where the cows and horses were kept.

Aunt Em dropped her work and came to the door. One glance told her of the danger close at hand.

"Quick, Dorothy!" she screamed. "Run for the cellar!"

Toto jumped out of Dorothy's arms and hid under the bed, and the girl started to get him. Aunt Em, badly frightened, threw open the trap door in the floor and climbed down the ladder into the small, dark hole. Dorothy caught Toto at last and started to follow her aunt. When she was halfway across the room there came a great shriek from the wind, and the house shook so hard that she lost her footing and sat down suddenly upon the floor.

Then a strange thing happened.

The house whirled around two or three times and rose slowly through the air. Dorothy felt as if she were going up in a balloon. [...]

Hour after hour passed away, and slowly Dorothy got over her fright; but she felt quite lonely, and the wind shrieked so loudly all about her that she nearly became deaf. At first she had wondered if she would be dashed to pieces when the house fell again; but as the hours passed and nothing terrible happened, she stopped worrying and resolved to wait calmly and see what the future would bring. At last she crawled over the swaying floor to her bed, and lay down upon it; and Toto followed and lay down beside her.

In spite of the swaying of the house and the wailing of the wind, Dorothy soon closed her eyes and fell fast asleep. [...]

She was awakened by a shock, so sudden and severe that if Dorothy had not been lying on the soft bed she might have been hurt. As it was, the jar made her catch her breath and wonder what had happened; and Toto put his cold little nose into her face and whined dismally. Dorothy sat up and noticed that the house was not moving; nor was it dark, for the bright sunshine came in at the window, flooding the little room. She sprang from her bed and with Toto at her heels ran and opened the door.

The little girl gave a cry of amazement and looked about her, her eyes growing bigger and bigger at the wonderful sights she saw.

The cyclone had set the house down very gently – for a cyclone – in the midst of a country of marvellous beauty. There were lovely patches of greensward all about, with stately trees bearing rich and luscious fruits. Banks of gorgeous flowers were on every hand, and birds with rare and brilliant plumage sang and fluttered in the trees and bushes. A little way off was a small brook, rushing and sparkling along between green banks, and murmuring in a voice very grateful to a little girl who had lived so long on the dry, grey prairies.

While she stood looking eagerly at the strange and beautiful sights, she noticed coming toward her a group of the queerest people she had ever seen. They were not as big as the grown folk she had always been used to; but neither were they very small. In fact, they seemed about as tall as Dorothy, who was a well-grown child for her age, although they were, so far as looks go, many years older.

Three were men and one a woman, and all were oddly dressed. They wore round hats that rose to a small point a foot above their heads, with little bells around the brims that tinkled sweetly as they moved. The hats of the men were blue; the little woman's hat was white, and she wore a white gown that hung in pleats from her shoulders. Over it were sprinkled little stars that glistened in the sun like diamonds. The men were dressed in blue, of the same shade as their hats, and wore well-polished boots with a deep roll of blue at the tops. The men, Dorothy thought, were about as old as Uncle Henry, for two of them had beards. But the little woman was doubtless much older. Her face was covered with wrinkles, her hair was nearly white, and she walked rather stiffly.

When these people drew near the house where Dorothy was standing in the doorway, they paused and whispered among themselves, as if afraid to come farther. But the little old woman walked up to Dorothy, made a low bow and said, in a sweet voice:

"You are welcome, most noble Sorceress, to the land of the Munchkins. We are so grateful to you for having killed the Wicked Witch of the East, and for setting our people free from bondage."

Dorothy listened to this speech with wonder. What could the little woman possibly mean by calling her a sorceress, and saying she had killed the Wicked Witch of the East? Dorothy was an innocent, harmless little girl, who had been carried by a cyclone many miles from home; and she had never killed anything in all her life.

The Wonderful Wizard of Oz, by L. Frank Baum

1 What is the name of the weather phenomenon that carries Dorothy's house to the land of the Munchkins?

_____

2 Why does Aunt Em tell Dorothy to 'run for the cellar'?

_____

_____

3 Why does Dorothy not make it to the cellar on time?

_____

_____

4 *... as the hours passed and nothing terrible happened, she stopped worrying and resolved to wait calmly and see what the future would bring.*

Which of these words is closest in meaning to 'resolved'? Tick **one**.

continued ☐

decided ☐

solved ☐

considered ☐

5 What kind of animal do you think Toto is? Explain your answer using **two** pieces of evidence from the text.

_____

_____

_____

_____

6 Read from *She was awakened by a shock* ... to ... *dry, grey, prairies*. Draw lines to match each of these words to their meanings.

jar		grass
greensward		feathers
plumage		stream
brook		jolt

7 Give **one** way that the Munchkins are similar to Dorothy and **one** way that the Munchkins are different from Dorothy.

_____

_____

8 Describe in your own words what the Munchkin men were wearing.

_____

_____

9 What does the little old lady call Dorothy that surprises her?

_____

10 Why are the Munchkins grateful to Dorothy?

_____

_____

Grammar in Action

Read from *Then a strange thing* ... to ... *in a balloon*. Find and copy **one** sentence that uses the subjunctive form (see page 6 for the subjunctive form).

_____

Traveller's Guide to the Solar System, by Giles Sparrow

This extract is from a non-fiction book that imagines what it would be like to be a space tourist in the future. It uses what we know about going into space to highlight some of the wonders and risks of travelling around the solar system.

Health advice

Long-duration space flight is a risky business, and despite all the advances in shielding and space medication, there are some factors you really need to keep in mind throughout your journey.

For one thing, you're going to be outside Earth's atmosphere for a long time. Insubstantial though our planet's air may seem, it's amazing how a couple of hundred kilometres of it can mount up, creating a far more effective shield than anything you could carry with you. Earth's magnetic field also helps to create a sort of protective cocoon.

However, once you're outside the atmosphere and beyond the magnetic field, you'll be prey to a wide variety of particles and high-energy radiations that zip around interplanetary space. A lot of them will pass straight through you, doing no harm at all, but occasionally one will make a direct hit on a cell, either damaging, killing or mutating it. Shields and medication can only do so much, and by keeping the bulk of your spacecraft between you and the Sun, you can reduce the danger to a minimum.

The other big risks come from prolonged weightlessness. While the initial side effects are relatively easy to get over, the long-term problems are harder to deal with. Muscles rapidly get weaker unless you exercise – on Earth, even the most dedicated couch potato is constantly doing exercise just to hold themselves up against gravity. After a few weeks in space, even bones get weaker – the lack of gravity scrambles the signals that tell them to keep renewing their calcium frameworks.

> Space pioneer Valery Polyakov spent more than 437 days on the Soviet space station Mir in the 1990s, suffering in the cause of space medicine.

Away from Earth, your blood no longer sinks towards your feet and ends up much more evenly distributed around your body. Unfortunately that cons your heart into thinking you've got enough oxygen in your blood already, so your body will reduce the number of new oxygen-carrying red cells it makes. It's not a problem in space, but land on any world with a half-decent amount of gravity and you'll risk fainting as your thinned-out blood makes a bee-line back to your boots.

The best solutions are regular exercise and, if possible, artificial gravity. Elastic shock cords attached to your belt can give you some 'gravity' to work against when you're on the treadmill or cross-trainer. Russian cosmonauts used to wear spring-loaded overalls that would fold up unless you constantly kept your muscles tense and there are still modern equivalents around. They're not to everyone's taste, though: one lapse in concentration, and you can find yourself in any number of uncomfortable and embarrassing poses.

> If you've got room for a treadmill on board, it'll help you keep in shape, though you'll have to strap yourself down before exercising.

Cabin fever

Before committing to a long-duration spaceflight, watch some reality TV! If you think the atmosphere gets bad when a bunch of strangers have been cooped up for a couple of weeks, think how much worse it could get with even less privacy, no escape, and the ever-present threat of cold, vacuumy death. Even astronauts with years of training and experience have been known to go a bit loopy, so pick your travelling companions carefully and use counselling software – it might feel weird confessing your inmost thoughts to a computer, but it's still better than flipping out and trying to evict someone through the airlock.

Space ailments

Long-duration spaceflight is not for hypochondriacs – you'll soon discover that you have more than enough real problems to worry about, without making up new ones. It's important to be in good shape before you go into space in the first place – there are plenty of problems that may seem minor on Earth, but can soon worsen with a dose of zero gravity.

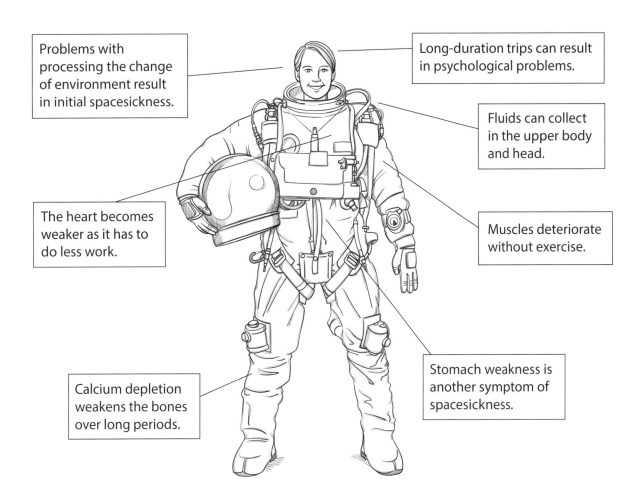

Problems with processing the change of environment result in initial spacesickness.

Long-duration trips can result in psychological problems.

Fluids can collect in the upper body and head.

The heart becomes weaker as it has to do less work.

Muscles deteriorate without exercise.

Stomach weakness is another symptom of spacesickness.

Calcium depletion weakens the bones over long periods.

Traveller's Guide to the Solar System, by Giles Sparrow

1. What **two** things protect you from dangerous particles and radiation when you are on Earth?

_____

2. Look at the paragraph beginning *For one thing ...* . Which word is closest in meaning to 'insubstantial'? Tick **one**.

unreal ☐   thin ☐

feeble ☐   transparent ☐

3. What are **two** ways of protecting yourself on a long journey through space?

_____

4. What was the name of the Soviet space station in the 1990s?

_____

5. Describe how your blood changes in space and why this change matters when you return to Earth.

_____

_____

_____

_____

6. How do astronauts exercise in zero gravity? Explain your answer using evidence from the text.

_____

_____

7. Why did Russian cosmonauts wear spring-loaded overalls?

_____

8 Long space flights can have a damaging effect on your body. Draw lines to match each cause to its effect.

radiation	psychological problems
weightlessness	damaged cells
lack of privacy	calcium depletion in bones

9 Look at the paragraph beginning *The other big risks ... .*
Find and copy **one** word that is similar in meaning to 'lengthy'.

_____

10 This extract uses a mixture of formal and informal language. Find and copy **three** examples of each into the table below. One example of each has been done for you.

Formal language	Informal language
insubstantial though our planet's air may seem	cold, vacuumy death

Grammar in Action

Tick to show the purpose of this text (see page 14 for the purpose of a text).

to inform you of the risks of a long space flight ☐

to explain what happens to your body when you are weightless ☐

to recount what has happened to astronauts on long space flights ☐

to argue that you should not travel for a long time in space ☐

The Way Back, by David Harsent

This poem was written by David Harsent about remembering a special time and place. The poet uses different senses to conjure up powerful memories.

Silence and nothing else brings you awake
In the night and you don't know where you are.
Go to the window, now, stare out at the dark,
How can you tell if it's near or far –
The light of a star in the lap of the lake?

How often have you looked at this photograph,
Edge with the glare of the morning sun?
A lake surrounded by firs ... Remember your laugh
Ringing the shoreline? Remember you won
In the echo competition? Remember how
Night was a long time coming, how you could row
Gently across, oars dipping light as a leaf?

Sometimes your shout would return to tease,
Mixed up with another voice. HELLO – Hello ...
Everyone wanted to try their special bellow
Like children lost in the woods. A mellow,
Lemony-scent came to you on the breeze.

The way back was through the pines
Or sometimes across the orchard, a short walk
Under a flawless sky. The fruit would fall
Cleanly into our hands, fresh from the stalk,
Hard and warm. We stuffed our pockets full.

To go there again, imagine the sky growing dark
And the evening star hanging low across the lake.
Stand by the window: away to the east
The tips of the pines are dissolving in mist.
Everything just as it was. Of lemons, only the aftertaste.

The Way Back, by David Harsent

1. Something unexpected wakes the poet up. What is it?

   _____

2. Look at the second verse. Describe everything that can be seen in the photograph.

   _____

3. As well as visual memories, the poet describes other memories using different senses. Find and copy **one** word or phrase from the poem for each of these senses.

   Sound: _____

   Smell: _____

   Touch: _____

4. Look at the fourth verse. Which of these words is a synonym of 'flawless'? Tick **one**.

   infinite ☐   entire ☐   perfect ☐   damaged ☐

5. How do you think the poet feels about the memories he recalls in this poem? Explain your answer using **two** pieces of evidence from the text.

   _____

   _____

   _____

   _____

Punctuation in Action

A lake surrounded by firs ... Remember your laugh
Ringing the shoreline?

Why do you think the author has used an ellipsis here (see page 22 for ellipses)?

_____

The Mouse and His Child, by Russell Hoban

A toy father mouse and his child are thrown away one Christmas. They become involved in some dangerous adventures, including a riot at a theatre, on their quest to become 'self-winding' (make their own decisions). In this extract, a bird has just picked them up and is carrying them away from danger.

The parrot's wings fanned gusts of cold air on the mouse and his child, and the darkness flowed by on either side. The moon had set; below them all was dim and grey. The father and son felt the wind race like a road unwinding underneath their feet as, motionless, they travelled on.

"I wonder what happened to Manny Rat," said the child. "I wonder if he got away."

"If he did, we can expect to see him again," said the father. "He seems determined to smash us, and I don't think he'll give up."

"Neither will we," said the child. "Will we, Papa?"

The father said nothing, and the child's only answer was the wind that whistled by them as they flew.

"We'll find the elephant and the seal, and we'll find the dolls' house too, and have our own territory, won't we, Papa?"

"You simply won't understand how it is," said the father. "How can we find anything? How can we ever hope to have our own territory?"

"But look how far we've come!" said the child. "And think of all we've done! We got out of the dump; we came through the war safely; we saved the Caws of Art."

"We escaped after the attempted bank robbery and survived the war only because we had Frog to help us," said the father. "And we saved the Caws of Art by making animals laugh at us. They laughed because we have no teeth or claws and can do nothing for ourselves. They laughed because we are ridiculous." Then he was silent, looking down at the child who hung from his arms in the darkness, the nutshell drum and good-luck charm swinging from his neck.

"Believe me," said Euterpe, "Crow doesn't think you're ridiculous, and neither do I. What you did was pretty clever, and it was brave too. You might have been smashed by that mob."

"Yes," said the father, "we're brave and clever – but not clever enough to wind ourselves up, unfortunately. If only we could!"

"Ah!" said Euterpe. "There's nothing you can do about that. Although, come to think of it, maybe there is."

"What do you mean?" asked the father.

"The beaver pond isn't far out of my way," said Euterpe. "Old Muskrat lives there. Ever heard of him?"

"No," said the father.

"Well," said Euterpe, "except for Manny Rat, he's the only one I know who can do anything with clockwork. He figures out all kinds of things." She changed course and swung north. "He's fixed broken windups for the Caws of Art once or twice," she said, "so maybe he can help you too."

"We're not broken," said the father. "Not yet."

"I mean, maybe he can fix you so you can wind yourselves up," said Euterpe. "I've heard he can do almost anything."

The parrot flew steadily on, and the child, hanging from his father's hands, now saw again the bright star Sirius. It seemed to fly onwards, keeping pace beside them through the distant sky. As before, the child found its light a comfort. His good-luck coin clinked against his drum, and now he felt luckier than ever before. "Maybe, we shan't always be helpless, Papa," he said. "Maybe we'll be self-winding someday."

"Maybe," said the father.

Below them, scattered houses and farms gave way to wooded hills, and the parrot flew lower. The trees came close as Euterpe swooped down to glide over a valley where a stream widened into a frozen pond. At one end of the pond was an irregular dam made of saplings and cut branches, and below the dam the ice-covered stream continued through the valley.

"That's the beaver dam," said the parrot as they flew over it, "and that big snowy mound in the middle of the pond is the beaver lodge. Muskrat has a smaller one right over there, and the entrance tunnel is somewhere on the bank. I think I see his tracks." She landed at the edge of the pond and set down the mouse and his child on the ice.

"Muskrat'll be sure to find you here," she said, "and if anybody can do anything for you, he can."

Father and son felt a wingtip brush them softly as Euterpe took off. "Goodbye and good luck," she said, and was gone.

The Mouse and His Child, by Russell Hoban

(1) Read the first paragraph of the story.

a. Find and copy **one** simile.

_____

b. Find and copy **one** word that is an antonym of 'mobile'.

_____

(2) What type of animal is Euterpe? Tick **one**.

a mouse ☐   a beaver ☐

a parrot ☐   a frog ☐

(3) Which character is a threat to the father mouse and his child? Explain your answer using evidence from the text.

_____

_____

(4) List **three** things mentioned in the text that the father mouse and his child have escaped from so far.

_____

(5) From his conversation with his child, describe how the father mouse is feeling. Explain your answer using evidence from the text.

_____

_____

_____

(6) What does the child mouse wear around his neck?

_____

7 The father mouse says:

"... How can we ever hope to have our own territory?"

"... we're brave and clever – but not clever enough to wind ourselves up, unfortunately.
   If only we could!"

Which statement best describes what the father mouse and child want? Tick **one**.

They want to be rulers of a country and to wind their own mechanisms up. ☐

They want somewhere safe to live and to be in control of their own lives. ☐

They want to buy somewhere nice to live and to be cleverer. ☐

They want a nice house and they don't want anyone's help. ☐

8 Why does Euterpe take the father mouse and his child to the beaver pond?

_____

_____

_____

9 What is the name of the mounds that both beavers and muskrats live in?

_____

10 Do you think the father mouse and his child will get what they want? Explain your answer using evidence from the text.

_____

_____

_____

_____

Grammar in Action

"Believe me," said Euterpe, "Crow doesn't think you're ridiculous, and neither do I. What you did was pretty clever, and it was brave too. You might have been smashed by that mob."

Underline the passive sentence in this direct speech (see page 4 for passive sentences).

National Animals, by Giles Clare

Many countries around the world use national symbols. Think of the red-and-white flag of England; St David, the patron saint of Wales; or the thistle, the national flower of Scotland. This non-fiction article examines why some countries choose national animals.

In addition to flags and flowers, many countries adopt certain animals – from the world-famous to the little known – as their national representatives. These animals may be large, eye-catching mammals, such as elephants, which are the national animal of Ivory Coast. In Belarus, it is the bison and Greece has chosen the dolphin to represent it. As well as mammals, national animals might also be birds. One of the most famous is the bald eagle in the USA. Some countries have fish (the black bream in South Africa), insects (the holly blue butterfly in Finland) or reptiles (the king cobra in India). Other places even have mythical creatures as their national animals. In Scotland, they have a unicorn; the Czech Republic has a lion with two tails; and in Serbia, they have a double-headed white eagle.

So, how do countries decide which animals, real or imaginary, should be their national symbols?

Some countries choose a creature to become their national animal because the creature is indigenous to that nation. Afghanistan, for example, is one of the few countries with a native population of rare and magnificent snow leopards living in the remote mountains. Go 'down under' and it is hard to think of Australia without thinking of kangaroos, or kiwis in New Zealand. Mention beavers and you are probably thinking of Canada. Giant pandas? China. Bulls? Spain.

Other nations have less eminent – but just as compelling – animals as their national symbols. Few people may be acquainted with the turquoise-browed motmot. However, the populations of El Salvador and Nicaragua celebrate it as their national bird. In Bhutan in the Himalayas, they have the takin. With the horns of a wildebeest, a tail like a bear and a moose-like nose, these 'goats with attitude' are revered as the national animal.

The most common national animal may not come as such a surprise. It is the mighty lion. Naturally, the king of the jungle is the national animal of many countries on the African continent, including Morocco, Kenya, Senegal and Cameroon. But interestingly, the lion is also raised to the status of national symbol in countries such as North Macedonia, Luxembourg, Singapore and England.

In fact, the lion has been chosen to represent 19 different countries around the world. Whilst an encounter with a lion is certainly more likely in Liberia than Bulgaria, for Bulgaria and other countries it is more about what the lion represents. In the past especially, such nations have been keen to look powerful, majestic or dominant – so what better than a lion? And if even a lion is not quite commanding enough, a powerful mythological creature might suffice instead, such as a Welsh dragon or a phoenix, the national animal of Lebanon.

Finally, amongst all these other animals, there is only one amphibian to make the grade: the Panamanian golden frog. It might only be a couple of inches long, but its skin is highly toxic. However, the frog is said to bring good luck as it supposedly turns to gold when it dies. In 2010, the government of Panama even passed a law recognising 14th August as 'National Golden Frog Day'.

Here are some fact files for some of the more unusual national animals from around the world:

Fact file 1: Komodo dragon
Country: Indonesia
Scientific name: *Varanus komodoensis*
Conservation status: endangered
Life span: 30 years
Diet: carnivorous hunter/scavenger

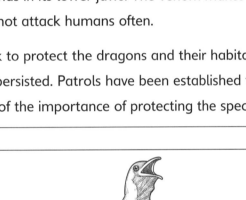

The Komodo dragon is the largest living lizard in the world. They can grow up to three metres long and weigh over 130kg.

A bite from a Komodo dragon can be dangerous as its saliva contains poisonous bacteria. In addition, a Komodo dragon has venom glands in its lower jaws. The venom makes your blood thinner and induces shock. However, they do not attack humans often.

In 1980, Indonesia established a national park to protect the dragons and their habitat. Unfortunately, threats to their habitats have persisted. Patrols have been established to prevent poaching and to persuade local communities of the importance of protecting the species.

Fact file 2: bare-throated bellbird
Country: Paraguay
Scientific name: *Procnias nudicollis*
Conservation status: near threatened
Size: 26–28cm
Diet: fruit

The bare-throated bellbird lives in the tropical and subtropical forests of South America. The male bird has bright white plumage and a patch of bare, blue skin around its beak and throat. The female is olive-brown with streaked yellow underparts.

The male has a piercing mating call that sounds like a hammer hitting metal. Remarkably, it is one of the loudest calls in the world, measuring around 125 decibels, which is louder than a chainsaw or a rock concert.

The bellbird plays an important part in dispersing seeds around the forest. It faces two main threats: loss of habitat and trapping by poachers for the pet bird trade.

National Animals, by Giles Clare

1 What is the national animal of the USA?

_____

2 What is unusual about the national animals of the Czech Republic and Serbia?

_____

3 *Some countries choose a creature to become their national animal because the creature is indigenous to that nation.*

Which of these words is closest in meaning to 'indigenous'? Tick **one**.

exotic ☐

domestic ☐

imported ☐

native ☐

4 Read the paragraph beginning *Other nations have ... .*

a. Find and copy **one** word that is similar in meaning to 'famous'.

_____

b. Find and copy **one** word that is similar in meaning to 'admired'.

_____

5 Which country has a strange-looking goat as its national animal?

_____

6 Some countries choose national animals that are not from the countries they represent. Give **one** example and explain your answer using evidence from the text.

_____

_____

7 Draw lines to match these animals to their nations.

bison		Senegal
king cobra		Belarus
phoenix		Lebanon
lion		India

8 What do the huge Komodo dragon and the tiny Panamanian golden frog have in common? Explain your answer using evidence from the text.

_____

_____

_____

_____

9 How does the bare-throated bellbird's diet help with the development of its habitat?

_____

10 What **two** threats do both the Komodo dragon and the bare-throated bellbird both face?

a. _____

b. _____

Punctuation in Action

Three of the birds in the text are named using hyphenated words. Write down these **three** compound adjectives (see page 20 for hyphens).

a. _____

b. _____

c. _____

Caged Bird, by Maya Angelou

Maya Angelou was a famous American poet and civil rights activist. This is one of her most well-known poems. In this poem, she uses a caged bird and a free bird to write about what oppression and freedom feel like.

A free bird leaps
on the back of the wind
and floats downstream
till the current ends
and dips his wing
in the orange sun rays
and dares to claim the sky.

But a bird that stalks
down his narrow cage
can seldom see through
his bars of rage
his wings are clipped and
his feet are tied
so he opens his throat to sing.

The caged bird sings
with a fearful trill
of things unknown
but longed for still
and his tune is heard
on the distant hill
for the caged bird
sings of freedom.

The free bird thinks of another breeze
and the trade winds soft through the sighing trees
and the fat worms waiting on a dawn bright lawn
and he names the sky his own.

But a caged bird stands on the grave of dreams
his shadow shouts on a nightmare scream
his wings are clipped and his feet are tied
so he opens his throat to sing.

The caged bird sings
with a fearful trill
of things unknown
but longed for still
and his tune is heard
on the distant hill
for the caged bird
sings of freedom.

Caged Bird, by Maya Angelou

(1) Look at the first two verses. Find and copy **two** lines that show the contrast between the experiences of the two birds.

Free bird: _____

Caged bird: _____

(2) *can seldom see through / his bars of rage*

Which adverb is similar in meaning to 'seldom'? Circle **one**.

frequently   irregularly   usually   rarely

(3) *But a caged bird stands on the grave of dreams*

What do you think this line means?

_____

_____

(4) How do you think the two birds feel? Explain your answer using evidence from the text.

_____

_____

(5) *for the caged bird / sings of freedom.*

These lines are repeated in the third and sixth verses. What do you think this shows about the caged bird?

_____

_____

Vocabulary in Action

The poem can be read as a metaphor (see page 36 for figurative language). Which of the following statements best describes the metaphorical meaning of the poem?

You must be allowed to make your own choices to live a full life. ☐

You can still have hope even when you are scared. ☐

The Girl Who Stole an Elephant, by Nizrana Farook

Chaya is a determined and brave girl who lives in the kingdom of Serendib – a historical name for the island of Sri Lanka. Chaya is also a jewel thief. At the start of her adventure, she has sneaked into the royal palace and finds herself in a little trouble ...

Chaya looked at the bronze spear pointing at her neck.

"Stop right there," said the guard.

Chaya took a step back and held up her hands. The linen pouch under her blouse clinked. The chatter of the crowds floated up from the promenade below, where the King's annual feast was taking place.

"What are you doing here, girl?" The guard waved the spear at her. From below them, the melody of the veenas drifted up. The musical show was starting.

Chaya shrugged, the pouch pressing against her chest. She rubbed her palms down her skirt and tried to keep her voice level. "I'm just looking around."

Her voice brought two more guards to the top of the stone steps cut into the hill. This was how the royal palace was built – a network of buildings at the top of the mountain, every rock and ledge forming courtyards and pools for the royal household while they ruled from above.

"You're not allowed here," the guard said to Chaya. "You should be down below, enjoying the food and festivities."

Not Chaya. She much preferred breaking into the Queen's rooms and stealing her jewels. There was a particularly nice blue sapphire in her pouch at that moment.

"Well?" The man jabbed his spear towards her. "What have you got to say for yourself?"

"I wanted to get a little closer to the palace. See what it's like. It looks so pretty from down there." She pointed in the direction of her village and made her face go all wistful.

The guard sighed. "Fine. Just make sure you don't do it again." He put his spear down. "Anything past the lion's entrance is strictly out of bounds to the public."

Chaya looked back and nodded meekly, as if noticing the giant lion statue for the first time, even though it could be seen from villages miles away. The stone stairway carved between the crouching lion's paws led into the complex of buildings that made up the inner palace.

"Come on now." The guard gripped her arm, making her wince. He pulled her to the cobbled walkway sloping downwards towards the celebrations below. "I don't want to see you here again."

The Queen's jewels jangled in her pouch. There were sapphires, tourmalines and star rubies set in heavy, shiny gold. How many jewels did one person need anyway? And these were just the ones from the drawer in the rosewood table by the bed. Pity she'd had to leave so quickly when she heard voices outside the door. And then to be seen when she was halfway down to the promenade was just bad luck.

She shrugged herself free of the guard and set off, her arm stinging from where his fingers had pinched her.

In spite of everything Chaya found herself gasping at the view from up there. The kingdom of Serendib spread out around her as far as the eye could see, thick green forests and strips of silver rivers, with the King's City below and clusters of little villages beyond.

But she wasn't ready to leave yet. Chaya paused near a tamarind tree and pretended to look up at the monkeys on it. Dappled sunshine prickled her face as she looked at the guard out of the corner of her eye.

He had stopped walking but was still watching her. She heard him swear loudly. "What are you doing now? Get out, girl, before I come and give you a thrashing."

The sensible thing to do was to get out of there as fast as she could. But the Queen's rooms were calling out to her. It was as if she could hear their whisper, right there in the warm sun. The softness of the velvet rugs, the gauzy bed curtains dancing in the breeze, and the promise of more riches within the ebony and teak cabinets.

Suddenly, a commotion came from above her, near the Queen's quarters. She heard shouting and the sound of people running.

[Chaya is pursued by guards through the palace]

Elephants from the temple stood on the lawn ahead of her, draped in their mirror-studded regalia, ready for the pageant later. In the middle of them stood the King's Grand Tusker, Ananda. He was wearing his special maroon and gold garments, and his tusks were massive and powerful up close.

Chaya ground to a stop on the grass and looked back. She was boxed in.

She sprinted up and ducked under the mighty bulk of Ananda, the world instantly going dark and dank. His mahout gave a shout and grabbed at her plait, yanking her head back, but she broke free and rolled out on the other side. She sprang up to see the mahout turn and yell at the guards thundering towards them, as some of the elephants had started to toss their heads alarmingly.

"Stop!" The mahout waved his arms at the guards. "The elephants are getting disturbed."

The guards slowed down and Chaya took her chance. She ran to the boundary and dashed out through the gates. She was free.

The Girl Who Stole an Elephant, by Nizrana Farook

(1) What event is taking place at the palace?

_____

(2) What instrument can Chaya hear?

_____

(3) _Chaya shrugged, the pouch pressing against her chest. She rubbed her palms down her skirt and tried to keep her voice level. "I'm just looking around."_

What does this tell you about how Chaya is feeling? Explain your answer using evidence from this part of the text.

_____

_____

_____

_____

(4) _"I wanted to get a little closer to the palace. See what it's like. It looks so pretty from down there." She pointed in the direction of her village and made her face go all wistful._

Which word is closest in meaning to 'wistful'? Tick **one**.

hopeful ☐   sad ☐

blank ☐   uncertain ☐

(5) Where did Chaya steal the jewels from?

_____

(6) Why doesn't Chaya leave the palace as quickly as possible? Explain your answer using evidence from the text.

_____

_____

7 How does Chaya realise that her theft has been discovered?

_____

_____

8 Draw lines to match each word to its meaning.

| regalia | | an elephant rider |

| pageant | | a piece of clothing |

| mahout | | a special set of clothes |

| garment | | a procession |

9 How is Chaya able to escape? Explain your answer using evidence from the text.

_____

_____

_____

_____

10 Do you think Chaya will steal again in the future? Explain your answer using evidence from the text.

_____

_____

Grammar in Action

The softness of the velvet rugs, the gauzy bed curtains dancing in the breeze, and the promise of more riches within the ebony and teak cabinets.

Sometimes a writer bends the rules of grammar for effect. What is unusual about this sentence (see page 8 for multipart sentences)?

_____

Amazing Evolution, by Anna Claybourne

This text has been written to explain how humans evolved. It describes some of the first steps in human evolution, explains how we know what happened millions of years ago and suggests some answers to common questions about evolution.

Here come the humans!

After the dinosaurs died out, a new group of mammals evolved. They were the primates, meaning 'leaders'. Scientists in the 1800s called them this because they include apes and humans, which were seen as the 'highest' or most advanced of living things. Today, the primates include lemurs, monkeys and apes.

How humans evolved

Is it true that humans are the most advanced of all living things? Well, evolution isn't a process of becoming 'higher' or more special. It just allows species to adapt to their surroundings. However, humans have turned out to be very unusual. We have the most powerful brains of any known species. And we're the only living things to have complex culture, art and technology, and written language.

The first primates developed about 55 million years ago, when some small, furry mammals evolved to live in trees. They developed hand-like feet for holding branches and forward-facing eyes. Somewhere between 13 and 7 million years ago, apes separated into two different branches. One of these evolved into chimpanzees, and one into hominins (humans and their ancestors).

The human family

From early hominins such as *Australopithecus*, a family tree of humans developed, probably in Africa. One branch evolved to become *Homo sapiens*, the modern human, between 300 000 and 200 000 years ago. We know there were several species of humans, but we're not sure how they were all related. Although there's only one species of human today, as recently as 35 000 years ago, different species of humans existed together and sometimes interacted with each other. Imagine what it would feel like to meet a different human species!

Why aren't we hairy?

Look at our closest living relatives, chimps and gorillas, and you'll see they're much hairier than us! As humans evolved, we lost our thick body hair. There are several theories about why:

- It helped get rid of disease-carrying lice and fleas.

- It helped us keep cool while running around hunting.

- It helped us to swim in water and catch fish.

Lucy

We have discovered a lot about how humans have evolved from the hundreds of fossils that have been unearthed. One of the most remarkable discoveries was made in 1974, in Ethiopia, east Africa, when two palaeontologists discovered the skeleton of a hominin who lived 3.2 million years ago. 'Lucy' is not the oldest hominin fossil to have been found, but she is one of the most complete.

Reconstructing Lucy

The bone fragments that the palaeontologists found made up 40% of a skeleton. This might not sound like much, but it's actually an amazing find. Often only a tiny bit of a skeleton is found, like a rib or jawbone. As apes are symmetrical, we can see what most of the skeleton would have looked like.

Cracking the clues

By studying Lucy closely, fossil experts have found out lots more about her, and about how humans evolved. We're still not sure, though, if Lucy's species evolved directly into modern humans. However, Lucy's skeleton gives scientists lots of clues about her. The bones shown in grey are the ones that were originally found. The white bones have been added.

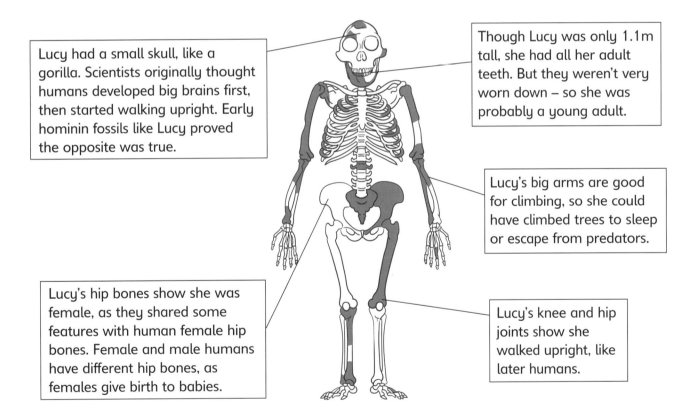

Lucy had a small skull, like a gorilla. Scientists originally thought humans developed big brains first, then started walking upright. Early hominin fossils like Lucy proved the opposite was true.

Though Lucy was only 1.1m tall, she had all her adult teeth. But they weren't very worn down – so she was probably a young adult.

Lucy's big arms are good for climbing, so she could have climbed trees to sleep or escape from predators.

Lucy's hip bones show she was female, as they shared some features with human female hip bones. Female and male humans have different hip bones, as females give birth to babies.

Lucy's knee and hip joints show she walked upright, like later humans.

Naming fossils

The team who found Lucy named her after a song they were playing at the time – 'Lucy in the Sky with Diamonds' by The Beatles. In 1978, Lucy and several other fossils were given their own scientific name, too – *Australopithecus afarensis*. And in Ethiopia she's called Dinkinesh, meaning 'You are marvellous'.

Amazing Evolution, by Anna Claybourne

(1) List **four** living mammals that are primates.

_____

(2) There are some ways that humans are unique compared to other species. Give **one** physical way and **one** social way.

Physical: _____

Social: _____

(3) How long have primates been on Earth?

_____

(4) What is the scientific name for modern humans?

_____

(5) Give **two** ways that scientists learn about the evolution of humans.

a. _____

b. _____

(6) Evolution allows species to adapt to their surroundings. Use the text to complete this table. Give **one** adaptation and **one** way that it helped each of these primates.

Primate	Adaptation	How it helped
first primates		
early hominins		
modern humans		

7 Put these events in human evolution in order from 1 (earliest) to 5 (latest).

development of complex culture, art and technology _____

apes separated into different branches _____

walking upright _____

several species of humans existed _____

development of big brains _____

8 Why could scientists find out lots of information from Lucy? Give **two** reasons.

_____

_____

9 Complete this fact file using information from the text. One section has been done for you.

Name	Lucy
Other names	
Location found	
Date found	
Sex	
Height	

10 Why do fossil experts think that Lucy was a young adult?

_____

_____

Spelling in Action

Look at the section titled **Lucy**. Find and copy **one** word meaning 'impressive', then write what type of word it is (see page 28 for suffixes).

_____

Comparing texts: the dark

Here are two texts. The first is an extract from a story called *Journey to the Centre of the Dark*, in which a boy is woken up in the night. The second is a poem called 'Dark Sky Park'. A dark sky park is a place where there are no artificial lights. Both texts deal with the same theme: the dark and our responses to it.

Journey to the Centre of the Dark, by David Machado

I was sleeping and I woke up when I heard my sister whispering to me. She's only five and I'm seven, so my main mission is to help her and teach her and protect her, and I go whenever she needs me. I opened my eyes but couldn't see anything. It was still night-time, and the room was really dark. I felt her hand on my arm and I asked:

"What happened?"

"A bad dream," my sister replied.

I remembered all the bad dreams I'd ever had, and a shiver ran down my spine.

"It's gone now," I explained.

"There were strange noises and shadows," my sister said.

"I know. But it's gone now," I said again.

"And monsters. Lots of monsters. Big ones and small ones and ones with claws and dirty teeth. They were ugly and horrible."

All of a sudden I didn't want to be there, talking to my sister with the light off. And I know I'm seven already, but even so, sometimes I still get scared. Especially of monsters. Of course, I didn't tell my sister that. I wanted her to believe I was brave and that she could count on me for anything.

"Wait," I said, "I'm going to turn the light on."

"You can't do that," my sister said, frightened.

"Why not?"

"Because of the monster."

"What monster?"

"The monster that's here next to me."

When she said that I was so scared my tummy hurt.

"There's no monster," I told her.

But, to tell the truth, I wasn't entirely sure. The darkness in the room was so black that, if there really was a monster next to my sister, there was no way I'd be able to see it.

"It's one of the monsters from my dream," she said. "It followed me and now it doesn't know how to get back to the other monsters."

Dark Sky Park, by Philip Gross

Now we're up on the edge
and over, on the mountain
with mountains beyond. Behind us,
    in the dark
of the valley, villages are embers
and the little city hugs its little glow,
ten miles away. Above,
    spark after spark
from a burned-out bonfire,
the stars spin away into space.
We huddle closer in our blankets, from the cold
    and the dark,
    in the dark
    of the dark sky park.

Tonight, look north, another edge
beyond this and ... can you believe
your eyes – that blue-green fraying
    of the dark
of space, like fine weed wavering
in a stream? Where the solar wind itches
the thin skin of our atmosphere, the faintest
    watermark
of light – just breathe the word: *Aurora*
Northern Lights – one that only appears,
and rarely, then, when held up
    to the dark
    to the dark
    of the dark sky park.

And us, where are we? On the edge
of the Earth. Are we riding this rock
bareback in the rodeo of stars? Or adrift
    in the dark
in a small boat on the open seas
of space, thrown together, refugees
with nowhere to go back to or
    to disembark?
Or picture this: a little boy out late
beyond the streetlights, dap-dapping this ball,
this one and only precious globe, alone
    in the park,
    in the dark,
    the dark sky park.

Comparing texts: the dark

1 In the story, why does the narrator's sister wake him up?

_____

2 Why doesn't the narrator in the story turn the light on?

_____

3 Which adjective do you think best describes the narrator's attitude towards his sister? Write **one** adjective and explain your answer using evidence from the text.

_____

_____

4 Who do you think is more frightened, the narrator or his sister? Explain your answer using evidence from the text.

_____

_____

_____

5 Find and copy **one** metaphor from the first verse of the poem.

_____

_____

6 Draw lines to match each phrase from the poem to the correct label.

| the solar wind itches the thin skin of our atmosphere | | simile |

| like fine weed wavering in a stream | | personification |

7 What rare natural phenomenon does the poet witness in the sky?

_____

8 Which statement best summarises the poet's feelings in the final verse? Tick **one**.

He is worried about where he is on the Earth. ☐

He is concerned about the refugees and the environment. ☐

He is overwhelmed wondering about his place in the universe. ☐

He is amazed by the size and scale of the universe. ☐

9 Both writers use the sense of touch to build an image in the reader's mind. Find and copy **one** example of this from the story and **one** from the poem.

Story: _____

_____

Poem: _____

_____

10 The narrator of the story and the poet feel differently about the dark. Explain how each one feels using evidence from the text.

_____

_____

_____

_____

_____

_____

Grammar in Action

Both writers use repetition to create cohesion (see page 12 for cohesion). Pick out **one** repeated group of words from the story and **one** repeated group of words from the poem.

Story: _____

Poem: _____

Writing skills: Space Story

The Writing skills task is inspired by the themes in the reading comprehension texts. It provides an opportunity to apply the skills practised in this book. Answer guidance can be downloaded from the **Schofield & Sims** website.

You are the captain of a spaceship that crash-lands on a planet. Records show that no-one has visited this planet before. Imagine your surprise as you stumble across a human settlement on the surface. Write an exciting short story for children your age about crash-landing on the planet and what you discover. Short stories usually have different stages, such as an opening, a problem, a climax and a resolution. Alternatively, you could leave your story on a cliffhanger to create suspense. Use the prompt below to begin your story if you wish to.

You could use some of the following in your short story:

- active and passive sentences (page 4)
- audience and purpose (page 14)
- colons (page 16)
- hyphens, ellipses and dashes (pages 20 and 22)
- figurative language (page 36).

Re-read 'The Wonderful Wizard of Oz' (page 48) and 'Traveller's Guide to the Solar System' (page 52) for some ideas.

"Everybody, safety belts on!" I shouted over the screaming alarm. "This is going to be rough!"

_____

_____

_____

_____

_____

_____

_____

_____

_____

_____

_____

_____

_____

_____

_____

_____

_____

_____

_____

_____

_____

Tip When you have finished writing, remember to proofread your story and correct any missing punctuation and spelling mistakes.

Final practice

The Final practice includes grammar, punctuation, spelling, vocabulary and reading comprehension questions. Work through the questions carefully and try to answer each one. The target time for completing these questions is 45 minutes. The answers can be downloaded from the **Schofield & Sims** website.

(1) Tick to show whether each sentence is active or passive.

Sentence	Active	Passive
a. The boy, who was artistic, was given a new set of paints for his birthday.		
b. At nine o'clock precisely, the captain ordered the crew to abandon ship.		
c. Two more days and all her problems would be solved.		
d. After fighting off the alligator, Charlie still had to face the anaconda.		

1 mark

(2) *She let the kite, which was a symbol of all her hopes and dreams, rise up into the air until it was just a speck.*

Tick to show which parts this multipart sentence has.

fronted adverbial ☐   relative clause ☐

adverbial of place ☐   main clause ☐

1 mark

(3) Underline the **two** synonyms in this sentence.

The football manager rued the team's missed chances, saying that he regretted

not making a substitution earlier.

1 mark

(4) Insert a colon and some semicolons in the correct places in this sentence.

The recipe requires several ingredients a knob of butter a pinch of salt

and pepper three egg whites, which should be whisked to a stiff peak

and one teaspoon of bicarbonate of soda.

1 mark

5 Rewrite this sentence using the correct spellings of the underlined words.

In her <u>corespondense</u>, my great-aunt recounted her <u>disarstrus</u> journey through <u>forain</u> lands <u>acommpanyed</u> by an <u>embbarasing</u> and <u>agrresive</u> donkey.

_____

_____

_____   1 mark

6 Draw lines to match the first part of each word to the correct ending.

pre		ible
convert		ably
unaccept		fer

1 mark

7 Tick to show where the missing semicolon should go.

☐   ☐   ☐   ☐
↓   ↓   ↓   ↓

My mum enjoys painting my aunt is more interested in photography.   1 mark

8 **a.** Rewrite this sentence using **two** hyphens in the correct places.

This week, we take an in depth look at the high octane adventures of a professional climber.

_____

_____   1 mark

b. Rewrite this sentence using **one** dash in the correct place.

It was too late to turn back would be dangerous and pointless.

_____

_____   1 mark

Final practice

9 Write the correct subjunctive form of the verb in brackets to complete this sentence.

If it _____ (be) up to me, we would go to the Caribbean

tomorrow for a holiday.

1 mark

10 Underline the correct spellings of the homophones in this sentence.

As we **past / passed** our old house, I was **effected / affected** by pleasant

memories of our lives there.

1 mark

11 *They have bigger fish to fry.*

What is this sentence an example of? Circle **one**.

simile   metaphor   idiom   homophone

1 mark

12 *I <u>guessed</u> that a (visitor) was coming to stay, but I couldn't work out who*
that (guest) might be.

a. Tick to show what the underlined words in this sentence are. Tick **one**.

homophones ☐   root words ☐

synonyms ☐   antonyms ☐

1 mark

b. Tick to show what the circled words in this sentence are. Tick **one**.

base words ☐   synonyms ☐

homophones ☐   derivatives ☐

1 mark

13 Underline the main clause in this sentence.

Not long before dawn, while the soldiers were still asleep in their tents, the

prisoner, who had spent weeks planning his escape, cut through the barbed wire.

1 mark

Final practice

The Devil and His Boy, by Anthony Horowitz

The Devil and His Boy is set in Tudor times. It follows the story of an orphaned boy called Tom Falconer. His adventures lead him to the streets of London, UK, where he meets some dangerous criminals.

Grimly had a yard at the end of a dark, narrow alleyway near the Thames. The city was much quieter here, with fewer people on the streets and a damp, evil-smelling fog in the air. Slimy water and mud rose over Tom's ankles as the two of them hurried towards a pair of mouldering wooden gates.

"My home," Grimly muttered. He opened the gates and ushered Tom inside. The gates led into a rough, partly cobbled courtyard, squeezed between three buildings that seemed to be leaning on each other to stay upright. Tom looked around him. Set in the middle of the courtyard was a single, wooden chair with a high back and solid arms and legs. Tom had no idea what the chair was for. But there was something about it that made him go cold inside.

"Belter!" Grimly called. "Snivel! Get the book! Get out here! We have a new recruit!"

Almost at once a door at the side of the courtyard flew open and two men hurried out. The first of these, the man called Belter, was huge and muscular, completely bald with a face that hadn't quite formed, like an over-sized baby. He was naked to the waist. He had no hair on his chest and his nipples were black. Snivel was older, a crumpled bag of a man, carrying a leather-bound book underneath his withered arm.

"A new recruit?" Snivel rasped. He licked his lip. "From Paul's Walk?" he asked.

"Where else?" Grimly turned to Tom. "We'll prepare you straight away."

"Prepare me?" Tom was getting more nervous by the second. "What do you mean?"

"I thought I told you. It's for charity!"

"Charity!" Snivel agreed.

"What sort of charity?" Tom demanded.

Grimly sighed. "The homeless and the disabled," he explained. "I've got boys all over London. On street corners. Outside churches. They're Grimly's boys."

"You mean they're beggars!"

"Exactly. But they're special beggars. They work for me and I take half of what they earn. But in return I help them, you see. I *adjust* them." Grimly flicked a finger in Tom's direction. "Take a boy like you. You're a little thin. A little ragged. But how much do you think that's worth? Good people, charitable people, people with money ... they want something more. Oh yes, they might give a penny to a child shivering in the cold. But how much do you think they'd give to that same child, *missing a leg*?"

Grimly had barely spoken the last three words before Tom was running for the gate. But Belter had been expecting it. Before Tom had taken two paces he was grabbed from behind and dragged, screaming to the wooden chair. There was nothing he could do as he was forced down, his hands and feet securely fastened with rope. It was over in a matter of seconds. By the time the giant had finished with him Tom was sitting helplessly, unable to move.

Final practice

"Let me go!" he shouted. "I've changed my mind! I don't want to work for you!"

Grimly touched a finger to his lips. "Don't shout," he said in a soft, soothing voice. "It won't hurt that much."

Belter had produced a dirty canvas bag from somewhere. He dropped it on the cobbled ground and Tom heard it clink.

"Now what shall we do with him?" Grimly asked. "How about one arm and one leg?"

Snivel had opened his book. "We did one of those last week," he said.

"All right then. Just the legs." Grimly smiled at Tom. "He's a handsome fellow. Interesting hair colour. Nice eyes. Let's leave the top half alone."

Belter grabbed hold of him and Tom screamed.

Then the doors of the yard crashed open.

Tom was too far gone to understand fully what was happening but he became dimly aware that Belter had straightened up again and that Grimly was walking forward with a look of annoyance on his face. "You!" he exclaimed. "What are you doing here?"

Tom forced his head to turn so that he could see the new arrival. A boy a couple of years older than himself was standing by the open door, leaning against the wall and smoking a pipe. He was looking at the scene with what could only be described as an amused smile. Tom thought he had seen the boy somewhere before but he knew that was impossible.

"Let the boy go," the new arrival demanded.

Final practice

14 Look at the first two paragraphs. Which word is closest in meaning to 'decaying'?

damp ☐   mouldering ☐

slimy ☐   cobbled ☐

1 mark

15 Explain how the writer builds tension in the second paragraph, using evidence from the text.

_____

_____

_____

_____

2 marks

16 What is Grimly's strong helper called?

_____

1 mark

17 *... a crumpled bag of a man ...*

The author uses this metaphor to describe Snivel. Thinking about this metaphor, describe what Snivel looks like in your own words.

_____

_____

1 mark

18 What is the name of the place where Grimly finds recruits like Tom?

_____

1 mark

19 Describe in your own words how Grimly's 'charity' works.

_____

_____

_____

2 marks

20 How does Grimly want to 'adjust' Tom?

_____ 1 mark

21 What do you think is likely to be in the 'dirty canvas bag'?

_____ 1 mark

22 How do you know the older boy is **not** a stranger to Grimly?

_____

_____ 1 mark

23 Compare Tom's feelings in this extract with the attitude of the boy who arrives at the end of the text. Explain your answer using evidence from the text.

_____

_____

_____

_____ 2 marks

24 What do you think is going to happen next in the story? Explain your answer using evidence from the text.

_____

_____

_____ 2 marks

Total:

30 marks